BIOGRAPHY FROM
ANCIENT CIVILIZATIONS
LEGENDS, FOLKLORE, AND STORIES OF ANCIENT WORLDS

The Life and Times of

JULIUS CAESAR

Mitchell Lane
PUBLISHERS

BIOGRAPHY FROM
ANCIENT CIVILIZATIONS
LEGENDS, FOLKLORE, AND STORIES OF ANCIENT WORLDS

**Titles
in the Series**

The Life and Times of:

BIOGRAPHY FROM
ANCIENT CIVILIZATIONS
LEGENDS, FOLKLORE, AND STORIES OF ANCIENT WORLDS

The Life and Times of

JULIUS CAESAR

Jim Whiting

Mitchell Lane
PUBLISHERS

Copyright © 2005 by Mitchell Lane Publishers, Inc. All rights reserved. No part of this book may be reproduced without written permission from the publisher. Printed and bound in the United States of America.

Printing   1   2   3   4   5   6   7   8
Library of Congress Cataloging-in-Publication Data

Whiting, Jim, 1943-
    The life and times of Julius Caesar / by Jim Whiting.
        p. cm. — (Biography from ancient civilizations)
    Includes bibliographical references and index.
    ISBN 1-58415-337-7 (library bound)
    1. Caesar, Julius—Juvenile literature. 2. Heads of state—Rome—Biography—Juvenile literature. 3. Generals—Rome—Biography—Juvenile literature. 4. Rome—History—Republic, 265–30 B.C.—Juvenile literature. I. Title. II. Series.
DG261 .W52   2005
937'.05—dc22
                                                                    2004024596

ABOUT THE AUTHOR: Jim Whiting has been a journalist, writer, editor, and photographer for more than 20 years. In addition to a lengthy stint as publisher of *Northwest Runner* magazine, Mr. Whiting has contributed articles to the *Seattle Times*, *Conde Nast Traveler*, *Newsday*, and *Saturday Evening Post*. He has written numerous books for Mitchell Lane in a variety of series. He has also edited more than 100 Mitchell Lane titles. A great lover of classical music and ancient history, he has written many books for young adults, including *The Life and Times of Irving Berlin* and *The Life and Times of Augustus Caesar* (Mitchell Lane). He lives in Washington state with his wife and two teenage sons.

PHOTO CREDITS: Cover, pp. 1, 3—Time Life Pictures/Getty Images; p. 6—Jamie Kondrchek; pp. 8, 12, 22, 30, 36, 38—Corbis, p. 10—Art History; p. 20—Library of Congress; p. 26—World History; p. 28—Hampden Academy.

PUBLISHER'S NOTE: This story is based on the author's extensive research, which he believes to be accurate. Documentation of such research is contained on page 47.

The internet sites referenced herein were active as of the publication date. Due to the fleeting nature of some web sites, we cannot guarantee they will all be active when you are reading this book.

BIOGRAPHY FROM ANCIENT CIVILIZATIONS

LEGENDS, FOLKLORE, AND STORIES OF ANCIENT WORLDS

The Life and Times of

JULIUS CAESAR

*For Your Information

This statue of Julius Caesar shows the confidence and the power he conveyed. He was nearly killed as a young man. He survived to become a famous general and important politician.

CHAPTER
ONE

A MAN OF HIS WORD

At the age of twenty-five, Julius Caesar was clearly an up-and-coming politician in the Roman Republic. He'd demonstrated personal courage during battle. He had become a successful lawyer who wasn't afraid to take on anyone. He was regarded as one of the city's best public speakers.

He decided to leave Rome and travel to the province of Asia, the western part of present-day Turkey. As his ship neared the island of Pharmacusa, a few miles off the Asian coast, he beheld a terrifying sight. Pirates, a common hazard in that part of the world, swooped out to intercept his ship.

Caesar's ship didn't have the manpower to fight back. Nor was it fast enough to escape. The pirates drew alongside and quickly swarmed aboard. Caesar's crew had two choices, neither of them very appealing. They could fight back. If they did, they would almost certainly be killed and dumped over the side. Or they could surrender and be sold into slavery.

The pirates immediately realized that Caesar was a member of a wealthy family. They decided to hold him hostage on Pharmacusa

Pirates have long presented a danger to seafarers. Caesar was fortunate to escape an encounter with them. The pirates in this illustration probably date from the 17th or 18th century.

and demand a sizable ransom. If the ransom wasn't paid, there was little doubt that he would be killed. In his biography of Caesar, ancient historian Plutarch calls these pirates "a set of the most bloodthirsty people in the world."[1] Facing a situation like this, most hostages would be terrified. Not Caesar.

The pirates told him that they would demand 20 talents for his release. Even though that was a considerable sum of money, Caesar laughed. A man of his importance was worth much more than 20 talents, he said. He told them to ask for 50 talents. The pirates must have been stunned. Some of their desperate captives had probably pleaded with them to reduce their ransom demands. Caesar must have been the first one to bargain upward. The pirates agreed to ask for the larger sum of money.

"Caesar was quite happy to do this, for he did not have to produce the money himself," writes modern historian Ernle Bradford. "Since they appeared not to be able to keep order in these territories, and since the pirates were obviously drawn from their own people and their cities flourished from this very piracy, the inhabitants of coastal Asia were under a strict obligation to

Rome to secure the release of any Roman citizen captured in their vicinity and, where necessary, to provide the ransom money."[2]

Caesar sent most of his servants to Asia to begin raising the money. Keeping just his personal physician and two servants, he settled down to wait. He knew that raising the dramatically increased amount of ransom money would leave him on Pharmacusa for an extended period of time. Pharmacusa is a tiny island, about two miles long by half a mile wide. Caesar acted as if he were the ruler of a little kingdom.

"With all the freedom in the world, he amused himself with joining in [the pirates'] exercises and games, as if they had not been his keepers, but his guards," Plutarch writes.[3] When he wanted to sleep, Caesar ordered the pirates to be quiet. He was just as dictatorial when he was awake. He often read his poems aloud and gave speeches. He required the pirates to listen to him. If any of them showed signs of boredom or didn't understand what he said, he insulted them. He even threatened to execute them. Everyone, including Caesar, got a good laugh out of his boldness. None of the pirates thought he was serious.

"They attributed his free talking to a kind of simplicity and boyish playfulness," writes Plutarch.[4]

There was nothing boyish about what happened more than five weeks later when the servants came back to Pharmacusa with the ransom money. Caesar was set free. Rather than sighing with relief and forgetting about the incident, he headed for the nearby port city of Miletus. He hired several ships and dozens of men, then returned to Pharmacusa. He overpowered the pirates and captured most of them. Along with their considerable store of plunder, he carried his prisoners back to the mainland. He traveled to visit the governor of the province, asking how the pirates should be

The city of Miletus was located on the western coast of modern-day Turkey. It was founded at about the same time as the Trojan War. It became an important trading center and thrived for more than 2,000 years.

punished. The governor said he would think about it. He probably wanted to sell them into slavery, rather than execute them. That would make money for him.

The governor's wait-and-see attitude didn't satisfy Caesar. He returned to the prisoners and took matters into his own hands. He ordered them to be crucified. Death by crucifixion is a long, agonizing process. At the last minute, Caesar decided to be "merciful." He cut their throats first. Then he crucified them.

Slavery in Rome

Slavery was a fact of life in many ancient civilizations, and Rome was no exception. According to some estimates, slaves made up at least one-third of the population. Probably the majority came from prisoners captured in battles. Pirates such as the ones who encountered Julius Caesar contributed many. Desperate, poverty-stricken Romans would even sell their own children as slaves.

Large landowners would have more than 4,000 slaves. While many slaves did backbreaking work in the fields, others performed highly specialized household tasks. "There were slaves to take care of each category of clothing, each kind of eating and drinking vessel, each kind of jewel, not to mention each stage of grooming, each kind of cooking, and every kind of service," according to Stephen G. Hyslop and Brian Pohanka.[5] The poet Seneca recorded that some had less glamorous jobs. "When we recline for dinner, one wipes our spittle, another picks up the scraps and crumbs thrown down by drunkards," he wrote.[6]

Many slaves lived in Rome itself as part of the city's ever-increasing bureaucracy. Others were physicians, tutors, and librarians. Some labored on public works projects. A few were selected as gladiators, who fought life-and-death struggles in huge stadiums to entertain crowds of people.

Treatment of slaves varied widely. Some owners were considerate. Others were inhumane, imposing whipping and branding.

Yet for nearly all slaves, there was a light at the end of the tunnel. Many were set free—when they became known as freedman. They could become Roman citizens, though they couldn't hold many political offices. Often their owners released them as a reward for years of faithful service. There was also an economic motive. Aristocratic Romans were not allowed to engage in commerce, but freedmen could. It was relatively common for members of the nobility to free a slave, then set him up in business and take a share of the profits.

Quaestors were elected officials during the time of the Roman Republic. They were especially concerned with overseeing financial affairs. Julius Caesar became a quaestor during his rise in Roman politics.

CHAPTER TWO

TURBULENT TIMES

Gaius (or Caius) Julius Caesar was born in Rome on the 13th of Quintilis (more than fifty years later, the month would be renamed Julius, or July, in his honor), probably in 100 B.C. His father was also named Gaius Julius Caesar, and his mother was named Aurelia. He had one sibling, a sister named Julia.

Though the boy was descended from a long line of aristocrats, his family wasn't as important as it had been at one time. His father was a member of the Roman Senate, but many other families were wealthier and had more influence on the city's affairs.

For several decades before Julius Caesar was born, two factions among the ruling aristocrats struggled for control of the Roman Republic. One was the Optimates, a conservative group that supported traditional values and wanted to keep power concentrated in the aristocracy. The other was the Populares, who wanted land reform and more rights for more people. Both sides often resorted to violence to try to advance their respective causes.

The Populares came to power a few years before Caesar's birth, when Marius became a consul, the highest office a Roman citizen could hold. Marius was responsible for changing the army from a militia—Roman citizens who took up arms only in times of emergency—to a professional standing army. With Rome continually expanding its borders, it was not uncommon for men to serve for more than twenty years. They were responsible for maintaining control in the far-flung lands that had come under Roman authority.

In 91 B.C., what was known as the Social War began. Nearby Italian cities that had supported Rome and were known as the *socii* ("allies") were pitted against Rome itself. The *socii* wanted the same rights and privileges that Roman citizens enjoyed. An Optimate named Sulla led the Roman armies and forced Marius into exile. When the Social War ended four years later, Sulla left Rome to lead a military campaign in Asia. Marius returned and helped the Populares take over the government. He died in 86 B.C. and was succeeded by Cinna, another Populare who had himself served four terms as consul.

At first, the political turmoil didn't have much effect on Caesar's life. He had the same type of upbringing as most aristocrats. A tutor—almost certainly a slave—taught him how to speak Greek, a language in common use among Rome's nobles. Caesar also studied grammar and literature. He wrote a poem praising the ancient Greek hero Hercules and a play about the tragedy of Oedipus. When he was thirteen, his father decided that it was time for his son to wear the *toga virilis*—the adult toga—the symbol that he had become a man. It was also the symbol of Roman citizenship.

Caesar's father died two years later. The teenager became the man of the family. By then he was engaged to a young woman named Cornelia, Cinna's daughter. When he was seventeen he married her, and within two years they had a daughter, Julia. His wife wasn't young Caesar's only link with the Populares. His aunt Julia had been married to Marius.

With these connections, Caesar would begin to face the harsh realities of Roman politics. Soon after the death of Caesar's father, Sulla returned from his campaign. Once again there was conflict between Optimates and Populares. It didn't last long, because Cinna was murdered by his own soldiers. Sulla led the Optimates to power. He wasn't afraid to use this power to advance himself and his party.

"While Sulla was addressing the Senate, the members were distracted by the rising sound of an uproar in the streets outside," write Hyslop and Pohanka. "According to Plutarch, Sulla simply 'bade the senators to pay attention to his speech and not busy themselves with what was going on outside: some naughty people were being admonished at his orders.' In fact, some 6,000 Marians [members of Marius's Populares] were being put to death."[1]

Almost literally overnight, Caesar went from a man with a bright future to a man who likely wouldn't have any kind of a future. Sulla had put out a hit list, and Caesar's name was on it. Even though many other men on the list were murdered, Caesar was spared. Sulla even issued a personal invitation for Caesar to join his party. There was one condition. He would have to divorce Cornelia and marry another young woman whom Sulla suggested.

Caesar turned him down. Enraged, Sulla put Caesar's name back on the list. Caesar had to flee and go into hiding. His lifestyle underwent a radical change, from pampered aristocrat to hunted fugitive. He came down with malaria and had to be carried from one hiding place to another. Once he was captured. He escaped by offering his captors more money than they would have received for bringing him in. He went back on the run. Finally several

Optimates who knew Caesar persuaded Sulla to remove his name from the list.

There was no telling how long Sulla's change of heart would last. He had serious misgivings about allowing Caesar to live. "Never forget that the man whom you want me to spare will one day prove the ruin of the party which you and I have so long defended. There are many Mariuses in this fellow Caesar,"[2] he told the men who had urged clemency for Caesar. In addition, Sulla had taken over the young man's property.

Not surprisingly, Caesar felt that it would be a good idea to leave Rome. He joined the staff of a general who was attacking the town of Mytilene on the island of Lesbos. Generals often took young aristocrats without military experience or training on to their staffs. In many cases, the primary function of these young men was to provide intellectual conversation for their generals; meanwhile, they'd have a chance to see a little bit of the world. Caesar was different. He was willing to do actual fighting. Eventually he was decorated with the *corona civica* ("civic crown," a wreath of oak leaves), which normally was awarded for saving the life of a fellow solider. The crown was more than a decoration. When a soldier wore one to public games, the spectators were required to stand as he passed them.

When Sulla died in 78 B.C., Caesar returned to Rome. He had been gone for four years. His ambition led him in the direction of politics. One of the primary paths to achieving public office lay through the law. Trials were often held in front of hundreds of spectators, who regarded them as a form of entertainment. Caesar took up a high-profile case, prosecuting a man named Gnaeus Cornelius Dolabella for corruption during his time as governor of the Roman province of Macedonia. As often happens today,

Dolabella hired the best legal talent to defend him. He was acquitted.

As Ernle Bradford points out, "Caesar had lost his first case, but he had achieved his main object: he had won great credit as an orator, and the very fact that the accused had felt himself in need of such eminent men to secure his acquittal added luster to Caesar's reputation."[3]

Soon Caesar was back in court. His opponent this time was Gaius Antonius Hybrida, who had used his position to plunder a number of Greek cities. Again Caesar lost, and again he added to his reputation. It was obvious that he was a rising star in the party of the Populares.

Improving his career led to his fateful trip when pirates captured him. Some people say that he was planning to sail for the island of Rhodes to study with a famous oratory teacher named Apollonius Molon. Others suggest that his money had run out. Many Greeks lived in Asia. Since Caesar's two high-profile legal cases had been in support of Greeks, it is likely that he was hoping to collect money from them.

Soon he was back on the battlefield. There was a revolt against Roman rule in Asia. Caesar raised some troops using his own money—much of which had come from what he had seized from his former pirate captors. He joined the Roman general who was fighting the rebels and campaigned for two years. Then he headed back to Rome.

He spent the next few years making an even bigger name for himself. Even in his twenties, he had his eye on becoming a consul. He knew what he had to do: make himself as attractive as possible to as many people as possible. As Plutarch notes, "He was very much in the good graces of the ordinary citizen because of his easy manners and the friendly way in which he mixed with people. Then there were his dinner parties and entertainments and a certain splendor about his whole way of life; all this made him gradually more and more important politically."[4]

When his aunt Julia died in 69 B.C., he gave a stirring public funeral oration that included plenty of praise of his own family. The crowd loved it. The Optimates looked at each other uneasily. Some of them may have remembered Sulla's words.

A few months later his wife, Cornelia, died. While most historians believe that he genuinely loved her, grief over her death didn't stop him from continuing to lead an extravagant social life. He dressed in the most expensive clothes, hosted parties that included several hundred guests, and spent a great deal of time in public. Soon he was elected as one of sixteen quaestors. These were magistrates who served in one of the Roman provinces for a year. This was an important stepping-stone on the way to higher offices.

His quaestorship was in the province of Further Spain (the south and southwest regions of present-day Spain). While he made some valuable political friends, for the most part he was bored. At one point he was even reduced to tears. According to Suetonius, another ancient historian, "He saw a statue of Alexander the Great and was overheard to sigh impatiently; vexed, it seems, that at an age [thirty-one] when Alexander had already conquered the whole world, he himself had done nothing in the least epoch-making."[5]

That was about to change. The next quarter century would be among the most epoch-making eras in world history.

The Roman Republic

According to legend, two brothers, Romulus and Remus, founded Rome in 753 B.C. In reality, there was probably a settlement at the site—on some of the hills on the Tiber River—long before that mythical date. For several centuries after its founding, the city was ruled by kings. An uprising in 510 B.C. expelled the kings. Rome became a republic.

The republic's power lay in the Senate, which originally consisted of about 100 aristocratic noblemen called patricians. Two of them were elected every year as consuls, who became the city's administrative and military leaders. Each man could veto the acts of the other. The Romans felt that this system would eliminate the absolute power of a king.

It didn't take long for the Roman Republic to expand. Nearby cities in the Italian peninsula quickly became part of the republic. Eventually it reached as far west as Spain and east to Greece and Asia Minor. Many of the new lands were won through battles. The main conflict was with the city of Carthage, located in present-day Tunisia in North Africa. The two sides fought three separate conflicts, known as the Punic Wars. Under the leadership of a brilliant general named Hannibal, the Carthaginians won several victories not far from Rome. But they were eventually repulsed. Rome finally defeated Carthage in 146 B.C. The city was burned, its ashes were plowed into the ground, and salt was poured into the furrows.

Hannibal

With the fall of Carthage, Rome became the largest, wealthiest, and most powerful city in the western world. Its size made the nation unwieldy. Its far-flung territories were increasingly difficult to rule. With so much power and wealth at stake, the city's leaders began to fight among themselves. Several were murdered by their opponents. This was the prevailing atmosphere in Rome when Caesar was forging his political career.

This illustration depicts Julius Caesar during one of his military campaigns. Several members of his staff stand nearby. Caesar enjoyed a reputation as an excellent commander.

CHAPTER

THREE

CONQUERING GAUL

When Caesar completed his one-year term as quaestor, he returned to Rome and remarried. His new wife, Pompeia, was the wealthy granddaughter of Sulla—the same man who once had threatened Caesar's life. At that time, the primary political question was who would command the Roman fleet that was going to finally put an end to piracy. The leading candidate was Pompey, a general who had a proven military record. Pompey was an Optimate, yet Caesar supported him.

Caesar further solidified his political base by supporting Crassus, a very wealthy Roman. Caesar became his closest assistant, managing many of Crassus's affairs. In return, Crassus loaned Caesar large amounts of money.

In 65 B.C., Caesar was appointed *curule aedile*. In this position, he was responsible for maintaining buildings, streets, and the extensive Roman sanitation system. More important for his political aspirations, he was also responsible for providing public games. Slaves performed nearly all of the menial tasks in Rome. As a result, the city was packed with poor people with a lot of time on their hands. They flocked to the public games, which included chariot races, mock sea battles, and gladiator fights. Caesar spent more money than anyone else had ever done on these entertainments. Most of this money was borrowed. He was taking a big risk. If he couldn't repay the money, he would be publicly humiliated and possibly forced out of Rome.

If he was worried, he didn't show it. Two years later his confidence had risen so much that he decided to run for the post of *pontifex maximus*, the chief priest of Rome. Two older men with excellent reputations were also running. It was a huge risk because a defeat could end his public career. Then, just as now, money proved to be a big help. Caesar outspent his opponents—again using mostly borrowed money.

According to Suetonius, he "used the most flagrant bribery"[1] in an effort to secure as many votes as possible. Financially, he was stretched nearly to the breaking point. "Reckoning up the enormous debts thus contracted, he told his mother, as she kissed him goodbye on the morning of the poll, that if he did not return to her as Chief Priest he would not return at all," Suetonius adds.[2]

He didn't have to worry. He won by a landslide. The position also brought with it another bonus: a much larger official home.

Caesar ascended to the next rung on the political ladder when he was elected as one of eight praetors, or state judges, in 62 B.C. When his yearlong term was over, he would become a provincial governor.

Soon Caesar found himself involved in a scandal. His wife allegedly had an affair with a young man named Clodius. Caesar proclaimed her innocence, but he still divorced her, saying, "I cannot have members of my household accused or even suspected."[3] Caesar's enemies, led by the famous orator Cicero and politician Cato the Younger, wouldn't let go. They brought Clodius to public trial and accused him of additional crimes.

The following year Caesar was able to escape from his increasingly demanding creditors and from the scandal when he became governor of the province of Spain. The appointment carried with it the chance to make a great deal of money from taxes and the spoils of war. That would enable him to get out of debt and put aside any further obligations to Crassus. When he was in Spain, he proved himself to be a skillful administrator. He also led his troops in successful military campaigns. He earned their respect and admiration by sharing the conditions they did, sleeping in the open and eating the same food.

When his term was up in 60 B.C., he returned to Rome. He

This is a statue of Clodius, who created a scandal when he disguised himself as a woman and entered Julius Caesar's home. He may have had a relationship with Caesar's wife Pompeia. Even though there was no definite proof of an affair, Caesar divorced Pompeia.

finally achieved his political goal by becoming a consul. A man named Bibulus was his co-consul, but Caesar had no intention of working with him. His careful cultivation of Pompey and Crassus paid off. Both men were unhappy with their treatment by the Senate. Pompey believed that he hadn't been honored enough for his leadership during battles in the East. The Senate refused to give Crassus a major military command or the financial benefits he requested. Even though he disliked Pompey, Crassus joined him and Caesar in an alliance known as the Triumvirate (which literally means "three men"). To further cement the alliance, Pompey married Caesar's daughter Julia (he was forty-six, Julia was about twenty-one), and Caesar married Calpurnia. She was the daughter of a close friend of Pompey's.

On the surface, the Triumvirate appeared to be an ideal team. It combined Pompey's outstanding military record, Crassus's immense fortune, and Caesar's oratorical skills and his popularity among the people. As events would reveal, having three men with such large egos would make for a fragile alliance. As usual, Caesar wanted more. With the example of Pompey in front of him, he realized that he had to become a successful general. Except for his relatively brief stints in Asia and more recently in Spain, he had virtually no experience commanding soldiers.

When his term as consul was over, he arranged to be appointed as governor of several provinces: Illyricum (the coast of Yugoslavia), Cisalpine Gaul (the northern portion of modern Italy), and—most important—Transalpine Gaul. The last was a huge territory, virtually unknown to the Romans. Much of it is in present-day France, and the word *Gallic* refers to the French.

Nearly all the inhabitants were nomadic tribes, many of them fierce and warlike. To oppose them, Caesar had the services of a number of Roman legions. Each legion consisted of 5,000 to 6,000 professional troops, heavily armed and very disciplined.

To make sure that everyone understood how great he was, Caesar recorded his military actions over the next eight years in *The Wars in Gaul*. In the book, he continually refers to himself in the third person. That way, it may not have sounded quite so self-glorifying. *The Wars in Gaul* also provides an important historical document. It reveals that Caesar was a brilliant military commander. Many times he made crucial decisions that were the difference between defeat and victory.

Caesar had other, more practical motives for going to Gaul besides self-glorification. One of the most important was that those nomadic tribes were a constant irritation at the border. Sometimes they would even invade Italy. There was a distant memory of a Gallic attack on Rome in 390 B.C.

Caesar didn't have to wait long to demonstrate his military ability. A large tribe, the Helvetii, wanted to move from their home in present-day Switzerland to get away from marauding bands of Germans. Part of their route lay in Caesar's new dominion. Even though the tribe's leaders told Caesar that they didn't want a battle, he refused to allow them to pass. His men were outnumbered but won a victory, killing thousands of the Helvetii. That impressed several tribes, who sent their leaders to Caesar to offer congratulations and assure him of their peaceful intentions. The following year, he won another victory over warriors known as the Nervii. When word of these victories got back to Rome, the Senate declared a fifteen-day period of feasting and thanksgiving.

Not everyone was happy. Pompey began to fear Caesar's growing military reputation. He was especially annoyed that Caesar's celebration lasted longer than the ones for his own victories. Pompey was also worried about Crassus. On several occasions, he charged Crassus with trying to assassinate him. Caesar too was becoming uneasy. He feared that Pompey might gain too much influence in Rome while he was engaged in fighting hundreds of miles away.

It didn't take long for the opponents of the Triumvirate to take advantage of the increasing dissension. The three men quickly realized the danger they were in. They met in secret and came to an agreement—for the time being.

Caesar soon had to rush off. A tribe on the French coast was causing problems. Caesar executed the tribe's leaders and sold everyone else into slavery. His actions were meant to serve as a warning to other tribes about the futility of fighting the Romans and

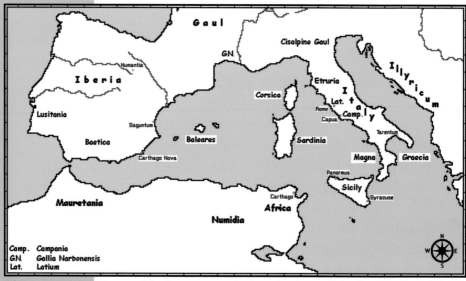

This map of the Western Mediterranean during the time of the Roman Republic shows the provinces for which Julius Caesar served as governor. His military campaigns in Gaul lasted for several years. They were of vital importance in establishing his reputation as a great military leader.

the consequences if they did. In the meantime, both Crassus and Pompey were reelected as consuls. Then they hurried off to fight, Pompey in Spain and Crassus in Asia.

Not long afterward, Caesar fought two German tribes. The fighting began with a skirmish in which a number of Romans were killed. In retaliation, Caesar not only defeated his enemies in battle but then set upon their women and children. Many were killed, while even more drowned as they tried to find safety by crossing the Rhine River. Caesar estimated that half a million people died in this incident.

In 55 B.C., he crossed the English Channel and mounted an invasion of the island of Britain. After overcoming some initial resistance, the adventure soon bogged down. The Britons staged a number of hit-and-run raids. Any Roman who went too far from camp didn't return. After less than three weeks, Caesar was forced to sail back across the English Channel. The next year he increased the size of his army and tried again. He was more successful, defeating the Britons in a battle. But after three months he realized that he would need far more men to maintain a permanent occupation. He withdrew. In military terms, the two incursions into Britain were of little or no importance. In terms of promoting Caesar, they were much more valuable. Caesar made it sound as if he won tremendous victories. That helped to increase his prestige back home.

He needed all the help he could get. Politics in Rome were not going well for him. As Caesar had feared, Pompey's power was increasing. The two men suffered a tragedy in 54 B.C. when Julia, Pompey's wife and Caesar's daughter, died in childbirth. Her death served to reduce Pompey's ties to Caesar, making him more dangerous.

Pompey wasn't the only source of danger for Caesar. In spite of Caesar's victories, Gaul was starting to slip away. One of his garrisons had been overwhelmed and all 1,500 men were killed. The Nervii nearly destroyed another. Caesar arrived just in time to save it and to prevent further defeats.

Thousands of miles away, Crassus was trying to match the military glory of his two partners. But he and most of his men were killed as they tried to invade Persia. It was the worst Roman military disaster in a century and a half.

Crassus had been the mediator between his two more powerful partners. Now that he was dead, the partners became even more suspicious of each other. Caesar proposed a deal: He would divorce Calpurnia and marry Pompey's daughter. Pompey would in turn marry Caesar's grandniece Octavia. Pompey turned down both offers.

Vercingetorix (mounted on a white horse), the leader of the Gauls, surrenders to Julius Caesar. Caesar is the figure in red, surrounded by his soldiers. This surrender marked the end of major fighting in Gaul.

Caesar's anxiety increased with still further trouble in Gaul. One reason for his previous successes was that he could fight the tribes one at a time. In addition, they had a strong leader named Vercingetorix (ver-sin-JET-uh-riks). Caesar managed to surround Vercingetorix and some of his troops in the city of Alesia. He knew that a huge army of reinforcements was on the way, so he constructed a double siege line with two sets of walls. One set faced inward and the other faced outward. Caesar defeated the reinforcements. Vercingetorix tried to break out but failed. He surrendered. Finally the rebellion was over, even though skirmishes would continue for another year.

It was a major triumph. Caesar had increased Rome's dominions by more than 200,000 square miles. Roman slave markets were crammed with thousands of his captives. Untold thousands more lay dead.

Roman Legions

During the time of Marius, the Roman army was opened to all citizens. It became a standing army of professional soldiers, most of whom enlisted for periods of twenty years or more. The basic unit was the *contubernium*. It consisted of eight men who shared a tent and cooking fire. Ten *contubernia* composed a century, which was commanded by a centurion. Six centuries were combined into a cohort. Ten cohorts formed a legion. Along with auxiliary personnel, that brought the number of men in a legion up to about 6,000.

Each legion was commanded by a legate. He was assisted by six tribunes. These were often inexperienced young men who were trying to gain military experience.

Each soldier wore a coat of light iron mail over a woolen tunic that reached to his knees. An iron helmet protected the top of his head, with large flaps on each side to cover his ears. Rather than boots, he wore sandals. These had thick leather soles with hobnails to give a good grip on grass or dirt roads. He carried a wooden shield about three feet high that was covered with leather. His weapons were the *pilum*—a weighted spear he learned to throw with deadly accuracy—and a short stabbing sword known as a *gladius*.

Each man was expected to carry enough gear to be almost entirely self-sufficient. His pack—which contained a bedroll, cooking and eating gear, a pickax and other tools, enough food to last two weeks, and more—was suspended on the end of a heavy stick that he carried over his shoulder. It usually weighed between 60 and 100 pounds. Despite this burden, legions commonly marched upward of twenty or thirty miles a day before making camp.

Gladii

Roman soldiers were tough, disciplined men. They fought together well, which was why they were able to defeat armies that were often much larger. When they retired from military service, they were usually rewarded with grants of land that provided a comfortable living for the rest of their lives.

Some Romans believed that Julius Caesar was becoming too powerful. A group of plotters murdered him on the floor of the Roman Senate. This illustration shows some men carrying his body away.

BIOGRAPHY FROM

ANCIENT CIVILIZATIONS

LEGENDS, FOLKLORE, AND STORIES OF ANCIENT WORLDS

CHAPTER
FOUR

CROSSING THE RUBICON

For Caesar, there was a dark side to all his successes. Soon he would have to yield his military command and return to Rome. That would make him vulnerable to legal attacks by the Optimates, who controlled the Senate. If he could hang on to his command long enough, however, he could run for consul. There was one problem. A candidate for consul had to live in Rome. Caesar was still in Gaul. He tried to receive an exception that would allow him to run while he was still in the field. Pompey and the other Optimates rejected the proposal.

By this time, the Triumvirate was only a memory. Crassus was dead; Caesar and Pompey had become enemies. In 50 B.C., bitter debates raged in the Senate about removing Caesar from command. No agreement could be reached. Meanwhile, Pompey began assembling an army of his own.

Early in 49 B.C., the situation came to a head. Mark Antony, one of Caesar's most trusted friends in the Senate, tried to read a letter from Caesar. According to the letter, Caesar said that he would give up his command if Pompey did the same. Mark Antony was shouted down. The Senate voted that Caesar would have to give up his command or be declared an enemy of the state. Mark Antony had to flee for his life.

Caesar believed that his own life would be in danger if he gave up his command and proceeded alone to Rome. With so many enemies in the city, he would almost certainly be put on trial, which likely would be followed by his execution. He made one of the most momentous decisions of his life. With a single legion of 5,000 men, he crossed the Rubicon, a river several miles south of the present-day Italian city of Ravenna. The Rubicon formed the boundary between his province of Cisalpine Gaul and Rome itself. That was an act of treason. Under Roman law, no provincial governor could command troops outside his dominion.

Caesar was completely conscious of the enormous step he was taking. He knew that he would plunge Rome into a destructive civil war. As his troops crossed the river, he said, "The die is cast."[1] Even today, the phrase *crossing the Rubicon* means to take decisive action from which there is no turning back.

He quickly proved both his genius as a military leader and as a reader of political trends. He divided his forces, sending half down the eastern shoreline of Italy while taking the other half on a more overland route toward Rome. His forces grew as they went. Many garrisons came over to his side.

He tried to summon Pompey to a peace conference and work out a compromise. Pompey realized that his troops were no match for Caesar's. Many of them were likely to cross over and support his enemy. He fled from Rome. Along with a number of senators, he made his way to the port city of Brundusium (present-day Brindisi). Though Caesar's rapidly moving troops nearly caught him, he managed to escape across the Adriatic Sea to Greece.

Caesar knew that his work had just begun. Pompey still enjoyed a great deal of support. In Greece, he was raising an army that was loyal to him. When he was strong enough, he would return to Rome and renew the conflict. Caesar faced another problem. He had to insure the steady flow of grain to the city. Much of it came from Spain, where a large army that remained loyal to Pompey could cut off the grain supply. He knew that he would first have to eliminate the threat from Spain. Then he could deal directly with Pompey.

Somewhat jokingly, he said, "I am going to fight an army without a leader, so that later I can fight a leader without an army."[2] He managed to accomplish the first half of his task without much loss of life. Then he returned to Rome and organized elections. He was elected consul. Since Pompey and most of the opposition had fled, the outcome surprised no one. In just over a year, the situation had changed 180 degrees. Caesar, not Pompey, was in control of the government. Pompey, not Caesar, was the outlaw.

Caesar set out after Pompey early in 48 B.C. Nine months later, even though he was outnumbered two to one, he defeated his enemy at the battle of Pharsalus, a plain in northern Greece. It was the largest battle ever fought between Romans. Thousands of men died. Caesar ordered that many of Pompey's officers be killed.

Pompey managed to escape the scene of the carnage. He fled across the Mediterranean Sea to Egypt. He hoped that he would be safe there. But his timing was terrible. Egypt was in turmoil because of conflict between its rulers, Ptolemy XIII and his sister, Cleopatra. Pompey was murdered before he could even set foot ashore.

A few days later, Caesar himself arrived. He wanted to add Egypt to the list of Roman provinces. He also decided to try to solve the differences between brother and sister. Ptolemy's supporters knew that their position would be weakened if Cleopatra could meet Caesar. They planned on murdering her before that could happen.

Cleopatra knew she was in danger. She decided on a ruse. She ordered her servants to roll her inside a rug, which was then carried past her would-be assassins, who were lurking near Caesar's quarters. The rug was unrolled in front of Caesar, who was immediately struck by Cleopatra's cunning and beauty. At fifty-two, Caesar began an affair with the twenty-one-year-old queen.

The Egyptians were enraged. Caesar controlled the palace, but his small force of 1,200 men was drastically outnumbered. At one point, Caesar was nearly killed when he temporarily left the safety of the palace. He had to swim for his life. Eventually Roman reinforcements arrived and tipped the balance in favor of Caesar. Ptolemy and many of his troops were killed in a battle. Cleopatra's position was assured. Soon afterward, she and Caesar sat side by side on an elaborately decorated barge as it made its way on a leisurely voyage up the Nile River.

Caesar left Cleopatra behind and returned to Rome. He probably also left behind a son. Most historians believe that he was the father of Cleopatra's child, Ptolemy XV, also called Caesarion, who was born not long after Caesar's departure. On his way back, Caesar fought a battle at Zela in the province of Asia. He sent a letter to Rome describing his victory there. The letter contained one of his most famous phrases: *Veni, Vidi, Vici* ("I came, I saw, I conquered").

Still more fighting was in store. Soon after returning to Rome, he had to battle an army in Africa that two of Pompey's sons and one of his former generals had assembled. After some initial reverses—by this time his legions contained a number of new recruits who weren't as experienced in battle as his longtime veterans had been—he won a major victory. That put him at the summit of his power and glory.

Cleopatra

Born in 69 B.C., Cleopatra VII became queen of Egypt at the age of eighteen on the death of her father, Ptolemy XII. She shared power with her twelve-year-old brother, Ptolemy XIII. In accordance with tradition, she married him. But they didn't get along. A few years later, Ptolemy XIII and his advisers managed to force Cleopatra out of the country.

With Caesar's help, Cleopatra regained her throne. Ptolemy died during the fighting. Caesar returned to Rome and Cleopatra married another brother, Ptolemy XIV. Then Cleopatra came to Rome at Caesar's invitation, accompanied by her son Ptolemy XV, nicknamed Caesarion (almost certainly Caesar was the father), and her brother/husband Ptolemy XIV.

With Rome in turmoil after Caesar's assassination, Mark Antony became suspicious of Cleopatra. He went to Egypt to see if she was helping his enemies. Just as she had done with Julius Caesar, she quickly seduced Mark Antony. He returned to Rome and married Octavia. She was the sister of Octavian, Julius Caesar's grandnephew and heir. Octavian was also one of Mark Antony's "partners" in the Second Triumvirate. Several years later Mark Antony went back to Egypt and married Cleopatra. Romans were outraged. Making matters worse, Mark Antony began giving royal titles to the children he had with Cleopatra. Octavian declared war.

The two sides met in 31 B.C. in the naval battle of Actium. Octavian won a decisive victory. Mark Antony and Cleopatra fled to Egypt, with Octavian pursuing them. Mark Antony committed suicide. Cleopatra was taken captive. She knew she would be taken to Rome and publicly humiliated. One day a servant carried a basket of figs past her guards. Concealed beneath the fruit was an asp, a highly poisonous snake. Cleopatra allowed it to bite her. On her death, Egypt became a Roman province. Even though Octavian was related to her son Caesarion, he knew that the boy would be a threat to his rule. He had Caesarion strangled.

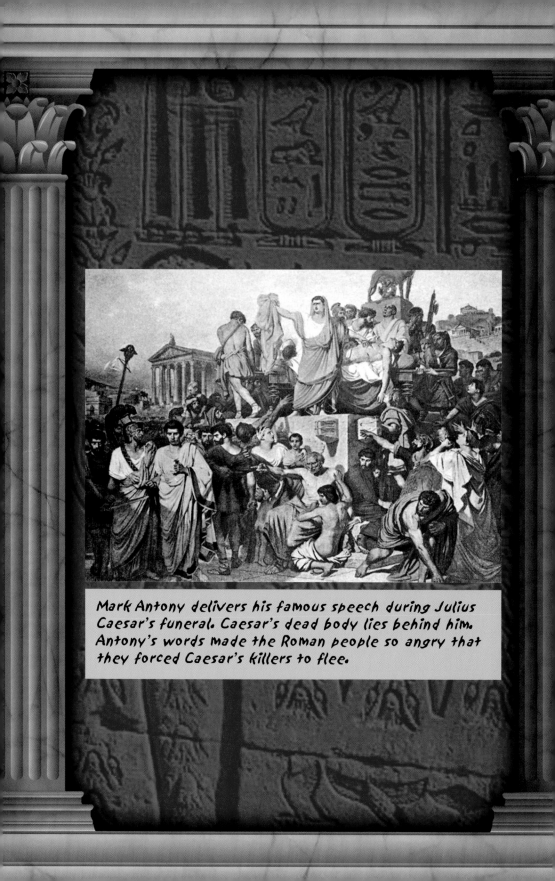

Mark Antony delivers his famous speech during Julius Caesar's funeral. Caesar's dead body lies behind him. Antony's words made the Roman people so angry that they forced Caesar's killers to flee.

CHAPTER
FIVE

THE IDES OF MARCH

Never one to be humble about his accomplishments, Caesar decided to hold an unprecedented four triumphs. There was one for each of his major victories: Gaul, Egypt, Africa, and Zela. The victory over Pompey at Pharsalus didn't count because it had cost the lives of fellow Romans. The city was packed with hundreds of thousands of spectators, who poured into Rome. They lived in improvised tent cities so they could attend these triumphs, which consisted of huge parades and other entertainments on a lavish scale. Caesar pulled Vercingetorix out of prison, hauled him in disgrace before the jeering population, then put him to death. Fittingly, Caesar brought up the rear of the parades.

Cleopatra and Caesarion made the long voyage from Egypt to take part. Cleopatra's presence may have made Caesar's wife, Calpurnia, uneasy. There were rumors that Caesar would divorce her and move to Alexandria, the capital of Egypt.

There was one final battle. The remnants of Pompey's army in Spain attacked Caesar's legions there. Once again, Caesar traveled to Spain to lead his troops. Although Pompey's forces achieved

This illustration shows Roman troops during a battle. Caesar stands in the upper right hand corner. His troops respected him because he was willing to share the same dangers that they faced.

some initial successes, Caesar's presence was enough to tip the scale in his favor. The rebels were defeated. Rome's civil war was finally over. Not surprisingly, Caesar also wrote a book about this conflict to make sure that everyone understood his point of view.

On his return to Rome, Caesar achieved a degree of power that no other Roman had ever enjoyed. His statues appeared all over the city. To many people, his exploits seemed almost godlike. Now that the threat of war had finally come to an end, Caesar turned his attention to administering the government. He began an ambitious road-building program. He wanted to erect large public buildings, including libraries and theaters.

One of his most significant achievements involved the calendar. For centuries, Rome had followed a system of calculating the length of the year on the basis of lunar months. That normally made a year about 355 days long. To make the year come out right, a short extra "month" was added. One problem with that system was that the priests who calculated the length of that extra period could be bribed, since so many terms of office were for a single year. Adding more days would make the term of office run longer than usual.

As the historian Suetonius explains, "[Caesar] reorganized the Calendar which the College of Priests had allowed to fall into such disorder, by inserting days or months as it suited them, that the harvest and vintage [grape harvest] festivals no longer corresponded with the appropriate seasons. He linked the year to the course of the sun by lengthening it to 365 days, abolishing the short extra month and adding an entire day every fourth year. But to make the next first of January fall at the right season, he drew out this particular year by two extra months, inserted between November and December."[1] As a result, 46 B.C. became perhaps the longest "year" in history. It had 445 days!

Known as the Julian calendar, this system wasn't changed until the sixteenth century. Many countries continued using it for centuries after that.

Some people became afraid of all the power that Caesar seemed to be concentrating. Rome was still a republic, and they feared that Caesar was trying to rule by himself. In public, at least, he made an effort to lessen those fears. On several occasions he refused a crown that Mark Antony tried to put on his head. He told the people that he was Caesar, not rex (king). These actions weren't enough to dispel the people's doubts.

In 45 B.C., small groups of men began meeting in secret. They were convinced that Caesar was too dangerous to remain alive. The leaders of this plot were Cassius and Brutus. They had both fought against Caesar at the battle of Pharsalus, but he had allowed them to live when they were captured. He was especially fond of Brutus, whom he appeared to regard almost as a son. That decision to spare Brutus's life came back to haunt him. After months of preparation, the conspirators decided that they would attack Caesar in the Roman Senate on the ides of March (March 15).

With so many men involved, rumors of the proposed assassination began circulating in Rome. Caesar's friends urged him to surround himself with bodyguards. A soothsayer named Spurrina encountered Caesar on the street and warned him to beware the ides of March. On the night of March 14, Calpurnia had a dream in which her husband was killed.

Caesar refused to pay attention to these portents. He went to the Senate as usual on the morning of March 15.

Spurrina was standing just outside the entrance. Historian Christian Meier writes, "Seeing him, Caesar smiled with an air of mocking superiority and said that the ides of March had come and nothing had happened to him. Spurrina replied, 'They have come, but they are not over.' "[2]

When Caesar was inside the Senate building, the conspirators surrounded him. One of them distracted Caesar by presenting a petition. At a signal, they pulled out concealed knives and attacked. Caesar warded off the first blow and grabbed the knife. But there were far too many enemies. He received twenty-three wounds as he crumpled to the floor next to a statue of Pompey. Waving their bloody knives, the conspirators ran through the streets proclaiming that Caesar was dead and the danger to the republic was over.

But they made a mistake. They allowed Mark Antony to speak at Caesar's funeral. In one of the most famous speeches of all time, he used the occasion to praise the fallen leader. He held up Caesar's bloody cloak and showed it to the spectators. They became inflamed with anger. Brutus and Cassius had to flee. Another man wasn't so lucky. Even though he had no connection with the plot, he had the same name as one of Caesar's killers. The enraged mob murdered him.

Two years later, an army led by Caesar's grandnephew Octavian and Mark Antony defeated Cassius and Brutus at the battle of Philippi. The two conspirators committed suicide rather than being captured. Octavian and Mark Antony, along with a man named Lepidus, formed the Second Triumvirate. It fell apart within a few years when Mark Antony met Cleopatra and became involved with her. Octavian defeated them in 31 B.C. and became the first Roman emperor. The republic was no more. Soon he took on the name of Augustus Caesar. Many people regard him as the greatest Roman ruler of all time. But it was the work of his granduncle that made Augustus's reign possible.

Author Phil Grabsky sums up the importance of Julius Caesar in these words. "As he had hoped, Caesar's legacy survived, not only for a few decades or centuries, but even to the present day. The very name 'Caesar' became synonymous with strong and powerful leadership. The Tsars, the Kaisers, the emperors who followed all took what was originally a family name and made it a symbol of their power."[3]

Julian Calendar

Well before Caesar's time, Romans had given the months of the year most of the names by which we know them today. Originally, Martius (March), named after their war god, Mars, was the first month. It was followed by Aprilis, Maius, and Junius (April, May, and June). The origins of those three names aren't as clear, though the latter two are likely named for the Roman goddesses Maia and Juno. Then came Quintilis, Sextilis, Septembris, Octobris, Novembris, and Decembris (based on Latin words for "five" through "ten"). These ten months totaled just over 300 days. An unnamed winter break of 50 to 60 days ended the year.

Eventually January (named for Janus, the gatekeeping god) and February (which probably comes from a word meaning "purification") were added, giving us our current twelve months. January was inserted at the beginning of the year, while February originally was the final month before being moved.

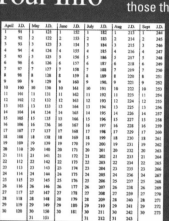

April	J.D.	May	J.D.	June	J.D.	July	J.D.	Aug	J.D.	Sept	J.D.
1	91	1	121	1	152	1	182	1	213	1	244
2	92	2	122	2	153	2	183	2	214	2	245
3	93	3	123	3	154	3	184	3	215	3	246
4	94	4	124	4	155	4	185	4	216	4	247
5	95	5	125	5	156	5	186	5	217	5	248
6	96	6	126	6	157	6	187	6	218	6	249
7	97	7	127	7	158	7	188	7	219	7	250
8	98	8	128	8	159	8	189	8	220	8	251
9	99	9	129	9	160	9	190	9	221	9	252
10	100	10	130	10	161	10	191	10	222	10	253
11	101	11	131	11	162	11	192	11	223	11	254
12	102	12	132	12	163	12	193	12	224	12	255
13	103	13	133	13	164	13	194	13	225	13	256
14	104	14	134	14	165	14	195	14	226	14	257
15	105	15	135	15	166	15	196	15	227	15	258
16	106	16	136	16	167	16	197	16	228	16	259
17	107	17	137	17	168	17	198	17	229	17	260
18	108	18	138	18	169	18	199	18	230	18	261
19	109	19	139	19	170	19	200	19	231	19	262
20	110	20	140	20	171	20	201	20	232	20	263
21	111	21	141	21	172	21	202	21	233	21	264
22	112	22	142	22	173	22	203	22	234	22	265
23	113	23	143	23	174	23	204	23	235	23	266
24	114	24	144	24	175	24	205	24	236	24	267
25	115	25	145	25	176	25	206	25	237	25	268
26	116	26	146	26	177	26	207	26	238	26	269
27	117	27	147	27	178	27	208	27	239	27	270
28	118	28	148	28	179	28	209	28	240	28	271
29	119	29	149	29	180	29	210	29	241	29	272
30	120	30	150	30	181	30	211	30	242	30	273
		31	151			31	212	31	243		

But the actual length of the year still varied. Many season-related festivals would occur at inappropriate times. Caesar wanted to make things more standard. Based on the solar year—the same system we use today—his new calendar gave 31 days to the odd-numbered months. Even-numbered ones had 30, except for February, with 29 days and 30 in leap years. In 8 B.C., Augustus Caesar—Julius's successor—had a month named for himself. It was Sextilis, the month following July (which had been named for Julius Caesar in 44 B.C.). Augustus Caesar felt that "his" month should have the same number of days as his predecessor's. He took one day from February and added it to August. To avoid having three consecutive months with 31 days, he decreed that September would give up a day to October, and November a day to December.

There was one more change to be made. Because the figure of 365 1/4 days per year is not precise, the Julian calendar contained an error of one day every 128 years. Pope Gregory made up for the discrepancy in 1582. He ordered that the day after October 4 would be October 15. To keep the discrepancy from occurring again, his calendar, called the Gregorian calendar, doesn't add a day in leap years that are divisible by 100 but not by 400. For example, the calendar added a day in the year 2000. It did not add one in 1900.

Chronology

(All dates are B.C.)

100	Born on Quintilis (later July) 13 in Rome as Gaius Julius Caesar
87	Begins wearing *toga virilis*, the sign of manhood
85	Father dies
83	Marries Cinna's daughter Cornelia
81	Daughter, Julia, is born; flees Rome
80	Is awarded the *corona civica* for personal heroism in battle
78	Returns to Rome
75	Captured by pirates; after being released, he returns and crucifies them
69	His aunt Julia and wife, Cornelia, die; serves as quaestor in Further Spain
67	Marries Pompeia, granddaughter of Sulla; votes to give Pompey total authority to fight piracy
63	Elected *pontifex maximus*, the chief priest of Rome
62	Elected praetor; after a scandal, divorces Pompeia for not being "above suspicion"
61	Wins first victories in Spain
60	Elected consul; forms First Triumvirate with Pompey and Crassus; marries Calpurnia
58	Begins campaign in Gaul (present-day France)
55	Invades Britain
52	Defeats Gaul leader Vercingetorix at the battle of Alesia
49	Crosses Rubicon River to begin civil war
48	Defeats Pompey at battle of Pharsalus; meets Cleopatra
47	Wins battle at Zela and sends letter with phrase *Veni, Vidi, Vici* ("I came, I saw, I conquered"); birth of son Caesarion (Ptolemy XV) by Cleopatra
46	Holds four triumphs in his honor; reforms the calendar
45	Adopts grandnephew Octavian as his heir
44	Murdered in Roman Senate on March 15

Timeline in History

146 B.C.	The Romans destroy Carthage, Rome's primary rival.
140	A famous marble statue of Roman goddess Venus is carved; 2,000 years later it will be called the Venus de Milo and displayed in the Louvre Museum in Paris, France.
133	Asia (present-day Turkey) becomes the eighth province of the Roman Empire.
107	Marius is elected consul for the first time.
106	Cicero, a famous Roman orator and politician who becomes one of Caesar's bitter political rivals, is born.
91	The Social War begins.
87	The Social War ends.
86	Marius dies.
84	Cinna, Cornelia's father, is murdered.
82	Sulla is appointed dictator.
78	Sulla dies.
71	A slave uprising led by Spartacus is crushed.
69	Cleopatra is born.
67	Pompey wipes out pirates.
63	Octavian, later known as Augustus Caesar, is born.
53	Crassus is killed in Parthia, a Persian province.
43	Cicero dies.
42	Brutus and Cassius, the two primary conspirators against Julius Caesar, are defeated in the battle of Philippi and commit suicide.
31	Octavian defeats Mark Antony and Cleopatra at the battle of Actium.
30	Antony and Cleopatra commit suicide; Egypt becomes a Roman province.
27	Octavian becomes the first emperor of Rome and takes the name of Augustus Caesar.
A.D. 8	Roman poet Ovid completes *Metamorphoses*.
9	Three Roman legions are annihilated in present-day Germany; the battle fixes the Rhine River as the northernmost point of the Roman Empire.
14	Augustus Caesar dies; his stepson Tiberius succeeds him.
37	Tiberius dies and Caligula, his nephew, becomes emperor.
47	Caligula is assassinated; Claudis I becomes emperor.
46	Greek biographer Plutarch is born.

Chapter Notes

CHAPTER ONE **A MAN OF HIS WORD**

1. Plutarch, *Plutarch's Lives*, translated by John Dryden, edited and revised by Arthur Hugh Clough (New York: The Modern Library, 1992), p. 200.

2. Ernle Bradford, *Julius Caesar: The Pursuit of Power* (New York: William Morrow, 1984), p. 39.

3. Plutarch, p. 200.

4. Ibid.

5. Stephen G. Hyslop and Brian Pohanka, *Timeframe 400 B.C.–A.D. 200: Empires Ascendant* (Richmond, VA: Time-Life Books, 1987), p. 63.

6. PBS: *The Roman Empire in the First Century*: "The Social Order," n.d., http://www.pbs.org/empires/romans/social/social5.html.

CHAPTER TWO **TURBULENT TIMES**

1. Stephen G. Hyslop and Brian Pohanka, *Timeframe 400 B.C.–A.D. 200: Empires Ascendant* (Richmond, VA: Time-Life Books, 1987), p. 69.

2. Suetonius, *The Twelve Caesars*, translated by Robert Graves (New York: Penguin Books, 1957), p. 14.

3. Ernle Bradford, *Julius Caesar: The Pursuit of Power* (New York: William Morrow, 1984), p. 35.

4. Phil Grabsky, *I, Caesar: Ruling the Roman Empire* (London: BBC Books, 1997), pp. 33–34.

5. Suetonius, p. 16.

CHAPTER THREE **CONQUERING GAUL**

1. Suetonius, *The Twelve Caesars*, translated by Robert Graves (New York: Penguin Books, 1957), p. 18.

2. Ibid.

3. Ibid., p. 45.

CHAPTER FOUR **ACROSS THE RUBICON**

1. Stephen G. Hyslop and Brian Pohanka, *Timeframe 400 B.C.–A.D. 200: Empires Ascendant* (Richmond, VA: Time-Life Books, 1987), p. 73.

2. Dupuy, Trevor, *The Military Life of Julius Caesar: Imperator* (New York: Barnes & Noble Books, 1996), p. 112.

CHAPTER FIVE **THE IDES OF MARCH**

1. Suetonius, *The Twelve Caesars*, translated by Robert Graves (New York: Penguin Books, 1957), p. 31.

2. Christian Meier, *Caesar: A Biography*, translated by David McClintock (New York: Basic Books, 1982), p. 486.

3. Phil Grabsky, *I, Caesar: Ruling the Roman Empire* (London: BBC Books, 1997), pp. 56–57.

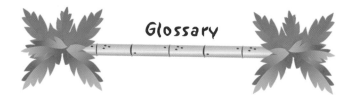

Glossary

aristocracy	(air-eh-STAH-kruh-see)—government by a small, privileged class.
aristocrat	(uh-RIS-tuh-krat)—a member of the aristocracy.
bureaucracy	(byoo-RAH-kruh-see)—administration of a government through several departments, or bureaus.
clemency	(CLEH-mun-see)—an act of mercy.
hobnails	(HOB-nayls)—short nails with thick heads driven into the soles of footwear.
mail	(MALE)—flexible armor consisting of interlocking metal rings.
orator	(OR-uh-ter)—a very skillful public speaker.
portent	(POR-tent)—something that foretells a coming event; an omen.
ruse	(RUZ)—a trick or ploy to escape the enemy.
solar year	(SO-lahr YEAR)—the length of time for Earth to complete a full revolution around the sun, consisting of 365.2422 days.
soothsayer	(SOOTH-say-er)—a person who makes predictions about the future.
triumph	(TRY-umf)—an elaborate public ceremony given in Rome to a general returning from winning a major battle in a foreign country.
vexed	(VEXT)—irritated, annoyed.

For Further Reading

For Young Adults

Bruns, Roger. *Julius Caesar*. Broomall, PA: Chelsea House Publishers, 2003.

James, Simon. *Ancient Rome*. New York: DK Publishing, 2004.

Morgan, Julian. *Cleopatra: Ruling in the Shadow of Rome*. New York: The Rosen Publishing Group, 2003.

Platt, Richard. *Julius Caesar: Great Dictator of Rome*. New York: Dorling Kindersley Publishing, 2001.

Works Consulted

Bradford, Ernle. *Julius Caesar: The Pursuit of Power*. New York: William Morrow, 1984.

Dupuy, Trevor. *The Military Life of Julius Caesar: Imperator*. New York: Barnes and Noble Books, 1996.

Grabsky, Phil. *I, Caesar: Ruling the Roman Empire*. London: BBC Books, 1997.

Hyslop, Stephen G., and Brian Pohanka. *Timeframe 400 B.C.–A.D. 200: Empires Ascendant*. Richmond, VA: Time-Life Books, 1987.

Meier, Christian. *Caesar: A Biography*. Translated by David McClintock. New York: Basic Books, 1982.

Plutarch. *Plutarch's Lives, Volume II*. Translated by John Dryden. Edited and revised by Arthur Hugh Clough. New York: The Modern Library, 1992.

Suetonius. *The Twelve Caesars*. Translated by Robert Graves. New York: Penguin Books, 1957.

On the Internet

Calendars Through the Ages: "The Early Roman Calendar"
http://webexhibits.org/calendars/calendar-roman.html

Calendopaedia—"The Julian Calendar"
http://www.geocities.com/calendopaedia/julian.htm

"Cleopatra VII, Ptolemaic Dynasty"
http://interoz.com/egypt/cleopatr.htm

Cross, Suzanne. *Julius Caesar: The Last Dictator*
http://heraklia.fws1.com/

The Glory That Was Rome—"The Roman Legion"
http://www.infohistory.com/rome.shtml#legion

Lendering, Jona C. *Julius Caesar—A Biography in 12 Parts*
http://www.livius.org/caa-can/caesar/caesar00.html

McManus, Barbara. *Julius Caesar: Historical Background*
http://www.vroma.org/~bmcmanus/caesar.html

PBS. *The Roman Empire in the First Century*—"The Social Order"
http://www.pbs.org/empires/romans/social/social5.html

Royalty Nu. *History of Egypt*—"Cleopatra VII, the Last Pharaoh"
http://www.royalty.nu/Africa/Egypt/Cleopatra.html

Index